Table of Contents

CHAPTER 1

Anything Is Possible!

The BASE jumper isn't scared. He stands at the **precipice**. That is a steep cliff. He jumps into the air. He drops down. He does a spin. Then he pulls his **canopy**. This is a special **parachute** for BASE jumpers. It looks like a bird wing. A parachute is a large device made of strong, thin cloth that slows a fall through the air.

BASE jumpers are similar to skydivers. They both jump from high places. But only skydivers jump from airplanes. BASE jumpers jump from fixed objects. That means the objects don't move.

The bird wing shape of the canopy helps BASE jumpers steer their way to a safe landing.

BASE stands for those objects: buildings, **antennas**, **spans**, and earth. Antennas are towers. Spans are bridges. "Earth" means jumping from structures in nature.

SHRED IT!
VOICE FROM THE FIELD:

Dean Potter and Whisper

Dean Potter had a miniature Australian cattle dog. Her name is Whisper. Whisper may be the world's first **wingsuit**-wearing BASE-jumping dog. A wingsuit is a one-piece outfit with webbing under the arms and between the legs that helps BASE jumpers fly. Whisper jumped from a 13,000-foot (3,962-meter) mountain. She and Potter were in the Swiss Alps. Potter created a special backpack to safely hold Whisper on his back. He did test runs with a stuffed animal. He made sure Whisper was okay with speed. He rode around with her on his bicycle and motorcycle. He drove about 80 miles (129 kilometers) per hour. Whisper even had her own goggles, or doggles.

Potter said, "Something almost made me crumble when I started putting the dog on my back. Nothing is going to happen to her. I'm ready. I'm not going to blow this flight."

A challenge for BASE jumpers is to jump from all 4 objects. BASE jumpers get a special number. Phil Smith did it. He was the first person. So, he is BASE 1. Carl Boenish created this system. He was the fourth person to do it. He is BASE 4.

BASE jumpers are always challenging themselves. They have to be daring. They have to be smart. They have to take chances. They have to jump.

In 1783, Louis-Sébastien Lenormand jumped from a tower. He was in France. He was testing his parachute. This was long before modern BASE jumping began.

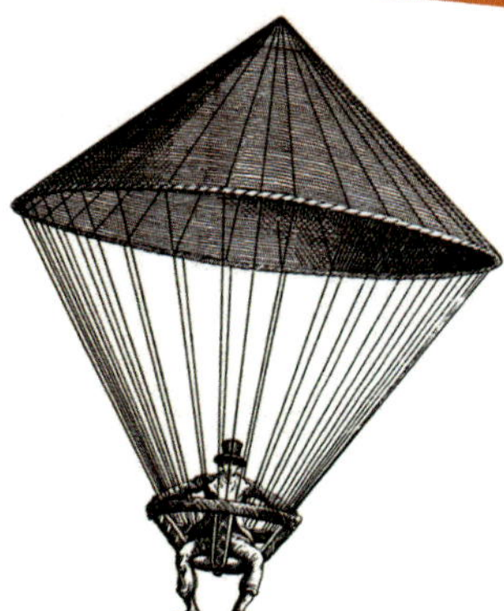

Fig. 62. — Parachute de Sébastien Lenormand (décembre 1783).

This BASE jumper opens his parachute after jumping from a high antenna.

CHAPTER 2

Free Fall Thrill

What could be more dangerous than skydiving? BASE jumping! BASE jumpers jump from lower heights than skydivers. Skydivers have more time to open a parachute. BASE jumpers only have a few seconds. Skydivers have sky around them. BASE jumpers risk hitting objects.

BASE jumping developed from skydiving. Skydivers wanted new challenges. Jumping from airplanes wasn't enough.

BASE jumping takes skill. BASE jumpers use their body. They control where they are going. They enjoy the **free fall**. This means falling with nothing slowing them down. They do this for as long as possible. Then they pull the canopy to start landing.

Many experienced BASE jumpers wear cameras to capture their adventures.

The canopy is different from skydiving parachutes. Skydiving parachutes are dome-shaped. A canopy is rectangular. It has handles. Jumpers use the handles to steer. This means BASE jumpers don't just dive. They glide, or fly.

BASE jumpers don't have backup parachutes like skydivers. They pack their canopies carefully. There can be no mistakes.

Some BASE jumpers wear wingsuits. These are designed to catch air. They help jumpers fly. There's webbing between the legs and under the arms. It makes jumpers glide like flying squirrels.

Wingsuits are dangerous. Even professional BASE jumpers and veteran skydivers are at risk of serious injury. There is a 1 in 2,000 chance that someone will die BASE jumping with a wingsuit. People work to make them safer. They love the thrill of the jump. Some have said it feels like they're flying like a bird.

EXTREME BASE JUMPING:
Know the Lingo

Aerial: tricks in the air

Chute: short for parachute

CRW: canopy relative work—moving two or more canopies close together while falling

Dead air exit: jumping from a fixed object; all BASE jumps start in dead air

FJC: first jump course

Flare: turn

Heading: reference point on the ground

Launch: the actual jump

PLF: parachute landing fall

Rig: equipment or gear

Running exit: running into the jump

Stack: a formation where canopies are stacked one on top of the other

Track: flying in a forward direction

DEAD AIR EXIT

CHAPTER 3

There's a BASE for Every Jumper!

BASE jumpers challenge themselves. Some prefer buildings or antennas. Some prefer spans or natural features. Some want to jump from them all!

BUILDINGS

BASE jumpers jump off buildings. Buildings need to be at least 50 stories high. This gives jumpers enough time to free fall. Then they open their canopies. Most jumpers jump outside buildings.

But some have jumped inside buildings. One man did a BASE jump inside St. Paul's Cathedral. This is in London. It's 225 feet (68.8 meters) tall.

TALL TV and RADIO ANTENNAS

BASE jumpers jump off tall TV and radio antennas. They must have permission from the owners. They have to be careful. They could get electric shocks.

BASE jumpers have jumped from the Eiffel Tower. The Eiffel Tower in Paris is an antenna. It is 1,083 feet (330 m) tall. BASE jumping from it is illegal.

SPANS

BASE jumpers jump from spans. Spans are bridges or natural arches. They cross valleys or waterways.

Idaho's Perrine Bridge is a popular BASE jumping spot. It is 486 feet (148 m) above the Snake River.

EARTH

BASE jumpers jump from earth. They look for high places. They jump from cliffs and mountains.

The Fisher Towers are tall red rocks in Utah. They look like towers. The tallest one is about 900 feet (274.3 m) tall! They are spiky. They are packed closely together. There are lots of dangerous winds. BASE jumpers have jumped off of them.

SCENIC OVERLOOK
STOP

SHRED IT!

Jonathan Cox

In 2023, **Jonathan Cox** set a new BASE jumping record. He completed 102 consecutive BASE jumps. He did it using **human-powered ascent**. That means getting to a jump spot on one's own. It means not getting help. It means not using a vehicle. Cox set his record by jumping from the Perrine Bridge in Twin falls, Idaho. This bridge spans Snake River Canyon. He would make the BASE jump, land, then jog on a trail back up to the top of the bridge. He did this 101 times! He stayed at the bottom after his final jump. The previous record was set in 2017 by Danny Weiland. He had made 64 jumps from the same bridge.

PERRINE BRIDGE BASE JUMP

CHAPTER 4

Keep Shredding!

Extreme BASE jumpers don't let anything stop them.

No Limits is an extreme sports team. Once they pretended to be priests. They hid their canopies under their robes. They tricked security. They made it into the Palace of Culture and Science. It's in Poland.

The Palace of Culture and Science in Warsaw, Poland

The team jumped off the top of it. It is 778 feet (237 m) tall! They landed safely. They sped off in a car. They got away.

In many places, BASE jumping is illegal. Illegal means it is not allowed by law.

BASE jumpers fight for places to jump. Some BASE jumpers have picked locks. They have climbed fences. They have tricked security guards. Some break laws.

BASE jumping is dangerous. People have died. Jumpers get trapped in their canopies. Canopies don't open. Or they open too late. Jumpers get hooked onto objects. They slam into objects. Jumpers drown after landing in water. Leave it to the professionals!

Places like construction sites are dangerous for BASE jumpers. But some think it's worth it!

The first BASE jumpers had to sneak into places. Police didn't want them to hurt themselves or others. BASE jumpers could go to jail.

Many take that risk. They think it is worth it. They want the thrill!

SHRED IT!

When Extreme Is Too Extreme!

Stanislav Aksenov has 2 passions. He enjoys BASE jumping and body piercing. He does not use a regular harness or straps. He hooks the canopy into the body piercings on his back. His skin holds up his body. His skin stretches under his weight. He did this stunt at 1,300 feet (396 m) above the ground. He jumped from high cliffs. He was in the Lauterbrunnen Valley. He dangled from the flesh of his own back. He did this for more than 2 minutes. He landed safely in a field.

BACK PIERCINGS LIKE STANISLOV AKSENOV'S

DID YOU KNOW?

- Before jumping, BASE jumpers drop a weighted ribbon to test the wind. They watch how the wind makes the ribbon move. If the wind blows toward them, it might push them into an object.

- An Australian man jumped from the Statue of Liberty. He noticed an open door. It led to the **torch**. This is a stick that can be set on fire and carried in one hand. The torch on the Statue of Liberty is fake. He was arrested afterward. He said, "I just couldn't help myself."

- Espen Fadnes tried to jump off the tallest building in Bangkok. He misjudged the landing. He crashed into a billboard. He fell onto the street below. He cut his left foot. He said the crash was "more embarrassing than painful."

- John Van Horne jumped from a tower. It's in Malaysia. It's 1,381 feet (421 m) high. He landed in a swimming pool. He landed in the middle of a pool party! It was on the roof of another tall building.

CONSIDER THIS!

TAKE A POSITION! Many places ban BASE jumping. Professional BASE jumpers are experienced jumpers. They have a lot of skills. They also use proper safety gear. Do you think they should be banned from places? Banned means officially not allowed. Argue your point with reasons and evidence.

SAY WHAT? Skydiving and BASE jumping have similarities and differences. Learn more about skydiving. Explain how these 2 sports are similar. Explain how they are different.

THINK ABOUT IT! Some professional BASE jumpers don't like people sneaking into places illegally. Luke Aikins is a member of the Red Bull Air Force. He has mixed feelings about the issue. He said, "One side of me is like, 'Oh cool,' and the other side is, 'Man, it's just going to make it harder for those of us trying to do it legally in the future.'" What do you think about this issue?

SEE A DIFFERENT SIDE! Imagine you are walking in a busy city. You look up. You see a BASE jumper flying at you. How would you feel about BASE jumping from this perspective? What safety concerns would you have?

LEARN MORE

BOOKS

Doeden, Matt. *BASE Jumping.* North Mankato, MN: Black Rabbit Books, The Creative Company, 2024.

Garrison, Hal. *BASE Jumping.* New York, NY: Gareth Stevens Publishing, 2018.

WEBSITES

With an adult, explore more online with these suggested searches.

BASE Jumping Facts for Kids | Kiddle

Red Bull Air Force

GLOSSARY

antennas (an-TEN-uhz) towers used to broadcast TV, radio, cell phone, or other signals

human-powered ascent (HYOO-muhn-POW-urd uh-SENT) when a person gets to the height they're jumping from without the help of any other person or vehicle

canopy (KAN-uh-pee) a special parachute for BASE jumpers that looks like a bird's wing

free fall (FREE FAWL) falling with nothing slowing one down; the time before a jumper opens their parachute or canopy

parachute (PA-ruh-shoot) a large device made of strong, thin cloth that slows a fall through the air

precipice (PREH-suh-puhs) a steep cliff

spans (SPANZ) man-made or natural bridges or arches that cover an opening

torch (TORCH) a wooden stick that can be set on fire and carried in one hand; the torch on the Statue of Liberty is not real

wingsuit (WING-soot) one-piece outfit with webbing under the arms and between the legs that slows free falls

INDEX